Yoga for Cats

TRAUDL & WALTER REINER

YOGA
for
CATS

VISTA

First published in Great Britain 1991
by Victor Gollancz Ltd

This Vista edition published 1997
Vista is an imprint of the Cassell Group
Wellington House, 125 Strand, London WC2R 0BB

A catalogue record for this book is
available from the British Library.

ISBN 0 575 60182 5

Printed in Italy by New Interlitho Italia SpA, Milan

97 98 99   10 9 8 7 6 5 4 3 2 1

For Friski, Boots
Jackie and Jed

"The regular practice of asanas, pranayama and meditation will lead you to become a sleek, fulfilled and wise cat."

– Swami Pussananda

Felix

May Ling

Scrappy

Sir Henry

We thank the Board of the Yoga-Cat
Institute for its friendly support.

Whiskers   Blackie

WARM-UPS AND PRE-EXERCISES

First, relax the paws and legs. Then follow with
the belly and chest, the neck, the face
and finally with the whiskers.

BACK EXERCISES

SHOULDER EXERCISES

Eye Movement Number One

Sit in a relaxed position. Keep your head still while following a moving object back and forth. Only your eyes should move.

SARVANGASANA

(Shoulder Stand)

Variation
(Bridge Pose)

SIRSASANA

(Head Stand)

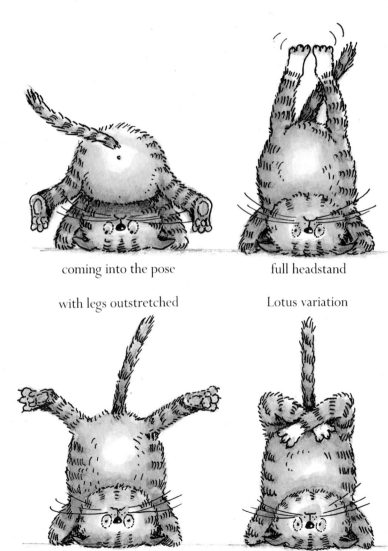

coming into the pose

full headstand

with legs outstretched

Lotus variation

Felix refreshes himself with a cold shower after his headstand
while Scrappy relaxes with comics.

VIPARITA KARANI

(Upside-down Pose)

HANUMANASANA

*(Splits,
or Hanuman Pose)*

HALASANA

(Plough Pose)

Steps

BHUJANGASANA

(Cobra Pose)

Variations

SALABHASANA

(Locust Pose)

Half Locust

Full Locust

DHANURASANA

(Bow Pose)

Ardha Matsyendrasana

(Half-spinal twist)

(Named after the
renowned
Yoga-master
Matsyendra)

Steps

Bent leg variation with paws
clasped behind back

full spinal twist

Mayurasana

(Peacock Pose)

Steps

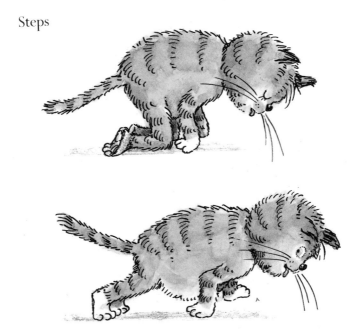

SUPTA VAJRASANA

(Recumbent Thunderbolt Pose)

Steps

JANU SIRSASANA

(Head-to-Knee Pose)

Steps

May Ling recovers after the Janu Sirsasana
exercise with meditation music.

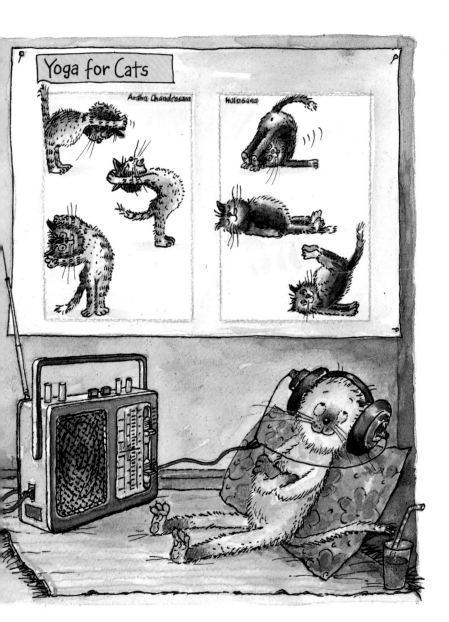

CHAKRASANA

(Wheel Pose)

Steps

KURMASANA

(Tortoise Pose)

Steps

CHATURKONASANA

(Four-Cornered Pose)

Variation

AKARNA DHANURASANA

(Shooting Bow Pose)

Step

Warm-Up

SAMKATASANA

(Heroic Pose)

Steps

MANDUKASANA

(Frog Pose)

Dynamic Variation

KUTILANGASANA

(Snake Pose)

Setuasana

(Full Bridge Pose)

SIMHASANA

(Lion Pose)

Variations

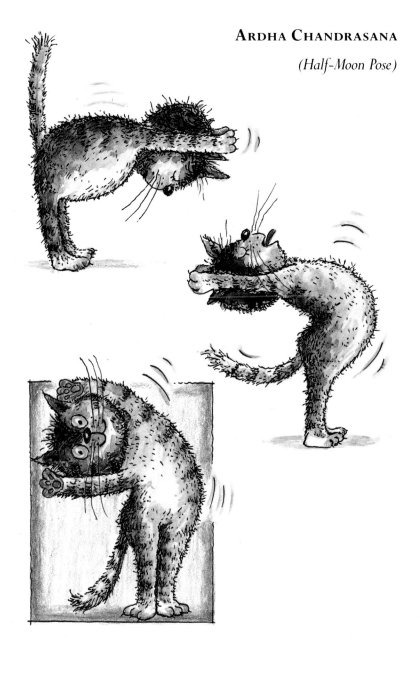

Sir Henry enjoys the break with his favourite reading.

GARUDASANA

(Eagle Pose)

Steps

Variation

Warm-Up

NATARAJASANA

(Lord of the Dance Pose)

Steps

Variations

TRIKONASANA

(Triangle Pose)

Steps

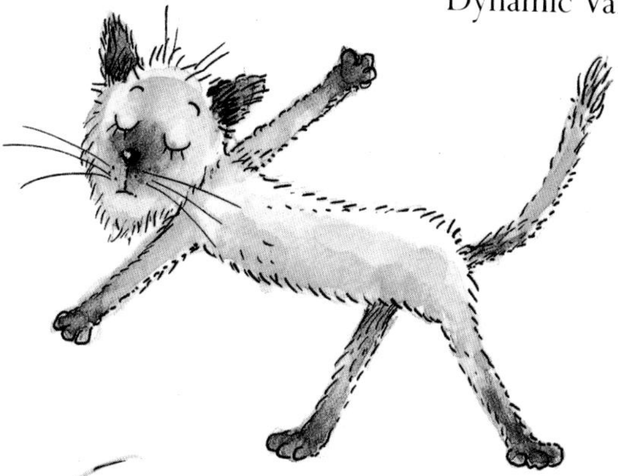

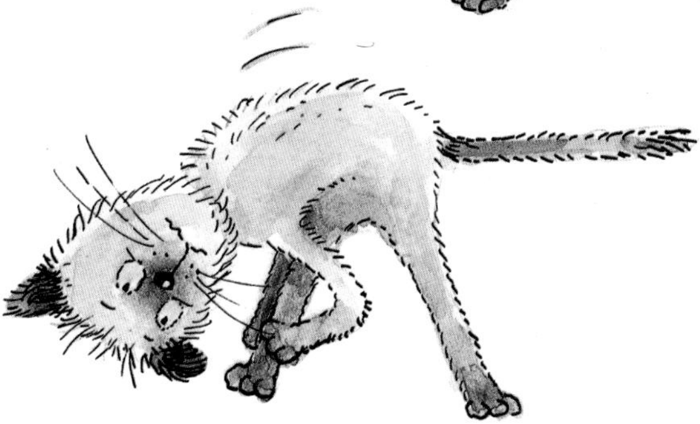

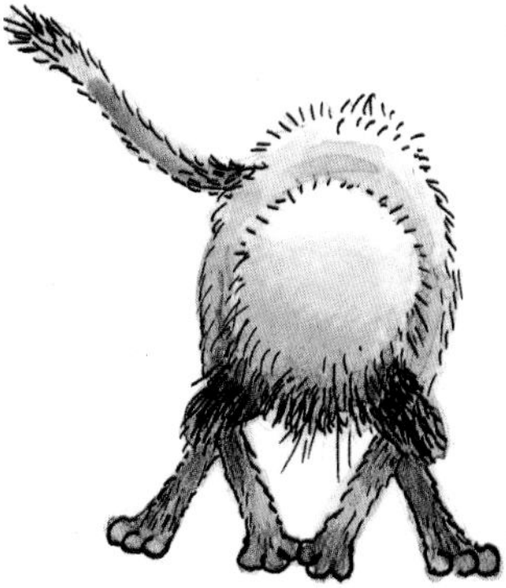

UTKATASANA

(Chair Pose)

BHADRASANA

(Gentle Pose)

SAVASANA

(Play Dead Pose)

Steps

MEDITATIVE POSES

(Full Lotus Pose)

VAJRASANA
(Thunderbolt Pose)

VIRASANA
(Warrior Pose)

SUKHASANA
(Relaxed Pose)

PADMASANA

(Lotus Position)

Warm-Ups

Blackie takes a break from training and relaxes
with the 'mouse programme'.

1. Variation

2. Variation

PADMASANA

(Lotus Position)

3. Variation

Yoga Mudra

(Tied and Bound Pose)

Steps

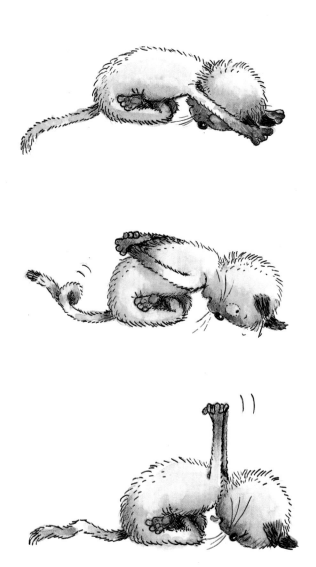

SURYANAMASKAR

(Sun Salute)

1 →

1 →

1 →

Whiskers' 'Sun Salute' during the break from training.

UDDIYANA BANDHA

(Stomach Hold)

Steps

MAHA BANDHA

*(Great Lock or
Chin Lock)*

Steps

MAHA VEDA

(Rooster Pose)

Variation

BREATHE DEEPLY

Warm-Ups

Press the diaphragm forward
and let the belly expand.

Exhale, draw in the diaphragm
and let the belly contract.

PRANAYAMA

*(Breathing
Practices)*

Steps

Alternate nostril breathing.

Other humour titles available in paperback: